I AM Worthy

By Veronda Ford

Published by Veronda Ford Enterprises LLC
©2014 Veronda Ford. All Rights Reserved.
ISBN: 978-0692410875

Edited by: Jewell Jackson

Contact:
www.verondaford.com
Veronda.Ford@gmail.com
(912)227-4212

Acknowledgments

I would first like to give honor to my Lord and Savior Jesus Christ through whom all things are possible. Through the guidance of the Holy Ghost, I was able to write my story that will prayerfully help others overcome by my testimony. I would not be the woman I AM today without the best mother in the world, the real MVP, Veronica Gamble. She is my rock, my foundation, and my mindset. To my number one fan, my husband, my middle school sweetheart, Johnny Ford, thank you for leading me on this journey of our lives. I can't transcribe the words to describe the joy, happiness, and genuine love you give to me. You make me better and push me to go higher.

Credits

To my editor, sister, and friend Jewell Jackson, you are a true gem, a jewel. You helped to take this book to the next level with your attention to detail, efficiency, and professionalism. You took my draft and turned it into a masterpiece that will inspire the world. To my cover designer Love McNill, you spent hours and hours revising, and reworking the graphics to ensure that my cover would make the best first impression to draw readers in to what is sure to be a life changing memoir. To everyone that has said or did something positive or negative to me, thank you from the bottom of my heart. You gave me the motivation to search within to find my worth. You are the reason for this book and I will forever be grateful. Thank you for the challenge. I would have never known just how worthy I AM, how much I AM loved, or how strong I AM if it wasn't for the challenge. I hope you take the challenge and come to realize just how worthy and deserving you are too.

Who is this book for?

Today I live in a world where many people seek validation in everything outside of themselves. Many people objectively assess their worth on things of no real value. Women want to be told they are beautiful by men. Men want to feel powerful and measure their greatness by the number of cars they possess and how much money they have. Children feel as though they have to compete with each other. Children who aren't the best dressed or the most athletic are bullied. Youth that feel outcast just want to be a part of something, so they join a gang to feel needed, to be loved, to belong and to feel worthy.

It is human nature to seek praise, to want attention, to want to be a part of something bigger than you. However, it does not have to come at the expense of your happiness and uniqueness. Young boys, young girls, kings and queens, don't look for validation and affirmation of who you outside of yourself when the great I AM that created you says YOU ARE. Just be.

This book is for every woman, every man, every child, and every person that has been or is at a point where you don't feel worthy, loved, valued, or noticed. You feel alone and as if no one understands or cares. I want you to know that you are never alone and you will never hit the bottom because God will reach all the way down, pick you up and settle you on high ground.

Be encouraged and know YOU ARE WORTHY.

You are worthy!

There are people in the world that will never be happy because they are not happy with themselves. Some people try to fill an insatiable void with drugs, houses, cars, children, spouses, parents, jobs, money, and food. The truth is only God can fill it because it was He who created it and knows the exact shape, size, and ingredients to put in it to make it complete. You are worthy because He created you for His glory and made you in His image. Nothing you can do can take away your worth because nothing or no one gave you your worth.

I AM!

I AM that I AM. Because the spirit of God resides within me, I possess the power and authority to be and do what I choose to. I AM limitless, constrained only by my own limitations within the boundaries of the Holy Ghost. I AM whatever I say I AM. I was created by the great I AM, Jesus Christ our God. His death allows me to live. His redemption allows me to be all that I AM created to be. His grace allows me to be all that I AM destined to be. Because God is, I AM. Without Him, I AM not.

The Story behind the Glory

I used to live my life trying to fit into what I thought was perfection. I was supposed to be the perfect child; well-mannered, respectable, and child who did not break the rules. I was supposed to get straight A's in school in order to guarantee my entry into the best colleges and become a reputable doctor. I was supposed to find my husband in college; one who was going to be a big shot lawyer or engineer. I was supposed to have the fairy tale story where we would get married, have twins, and live happily ever after in our house with the white picket fence. At least this is what I thought.

For a while, I did everything in MY power to make sure that my life happened that way. When life didn't happen as planned, I did my best to cover it up, to pretend that nothing was wrong. Truthfully, I could only "fake it until I make it" for so long. Eventually, the truth comes to light. Everything held under wraps erupted. In the process, I had become something I was not while trying to live up to what I thought was "the standard" of being worthy.

One day it hit me. I could never reach "the standard". I made a god out of trying to live up to my own standard when all along, God was calling me to live up to His standard. I had put my all and everything into creating this persona, life, and image that just did not fit the picture. I had finally come to a point where I was left with only myself. Mistakenly, I was trying to put together the pieces of a puzzle that God designed, erroneously using my own prototype. I did not understand that God had a map for me far greater than I could imagine if only I was willing to remove my own small and feeble plans out of the way. I just did not get it then but I knew it was more required of me because it had been planted in me from childhood. I decided to take the challenge and figure it out. I decided: I do not want to be what I AM not. I decided, I had to know who I AM.

I had become so overwhelmed with being the "strong woman". I was tired of bearing the burden of my life alone. I was tired of not having anyone to turn to when I needed them most. Well, let me clarify. It definitely was not the fact that I did not have anyone to turn to; I just chose not to disclose my trials and tribulations to anyone out of fear of being judged, ridiculed, or receiving bad advice. Everyone does not have wise counsel. Some people may have good intentions but not on all subject matters. In this instance, I had to encourage myself. I had to guard my heart and protect the truth from being distorted by the public and critics awaiting my downfall. By this I mean I had to keep my business to myself because when the storm is over, some people still like to rain on your parade. Some people never forget and hold you to something that happened in the past. Ultimately I had to come to the point where only GOD, the great I AM, could see me through. He wanted me totally dependent upon Him and only Him.

The Challenge

For thirty days, I decided to forsake all others. I totally immersed myself in the safe refuge and strength of God. I retreated from society. I purged myself of people's expectations. I did not lean on validation from others. I also purged myself of my own harsh expectations.

Sometimes I AM my own worst critic, often comparing myself to what I think I should be doing or what I should have accomplished, without taking into account the obstacles, barriers, and blocks I had overcome to get to where I AM.

I took the time to train my brain to applaud myself instead of sabotaging myself. Each day I told myself that I AM worthy of everything good. I told myself that even in the eye of the storm, even in the face of bad things, I AM deserving of everything good. I told myself that I must walk in that daily in order to turn the trajectory around that I was on. Some days, it was definitely hard to believe what I was saying to myself, but I affirmed it, read and said it until I acted on it, and then I came to believe it.

From the first day and everyday thereafter, my new found way of thinking became a part of my makeup. Every day, something was said or something happened that affirmed the positive of who I AM. I chose to embrace that. If on any given day, something negative happened, I mentally flipped the situation around. I told myself, I AM the opposite of whatever the situation was. With this pattern I broke the negative talk. That initial thirty day process helped me to grow and mature.

I kept a journal of my experiences; each day writing out the positive moment that I wanted to dwell on throughout the day. The thirty day I AM Challenge of affirming myself birthed I AM moments that changed my life.

Father God in the Name of Jesus,

I pray that every person that reads this book finds You, the truth, making you their Lord and Savior, redeeming them from the bottom of their situation and taking them to new levels, new understanding, and a new self. Open their eyes to truth, transform their hearts that they yearn and long for You. Give them hope, joy, and reveal their worth. You so loved the world that you gave your only begotten son proving our worth. I ask that you bring these words to life so that your will be done in our lives.

In Jesus name I pray, Amen.

DAY 1

I AM Worthy!

Worthy = Deserving of effort, attention or respect
You are a person of distinguished merit, value, and
importance. You are worthy!

Today I decided that in all that I go through I have to fully rely on God and not look for my worth in anyone or anything else. In all, I AM worthy of all things good and no one or nothing can stop me from getting what is mine. I was tired of fighting and not winning. I was tired of giving and not gaining. I started this I AM challenge because I needed to find me again. I often reflect back on my life and often think to walk a mile in my shoes you need to stretch, prep, pray, get water, and take a boot camp. Sometimes, I think if it wasn't by the strength of God, I couldn't even walk in my own shoes. I AM where I AM because of God and I will always give him the honor, glory and praise. He saw in me what others didn't and what I didn't even see in myself. At times I still don't see anything so great. When I think about the fact that his blood was shed for me, I can't help but realize how precious I AM, how worthy I AM that he died to save me. He died for us all. For that reason alone I find power to live up to my worth, knowing I deserve the best, I AM chosen, and I AM destined for great things.

I AM WORTHY!

DAY 2

I AM Loved!

Loved = To be adored, to have a warm personal attraction or deep affection

You don't need the world when you have someone that thinks the world of you!

Today my family and I had a nice home cooked dinner together. When it comes to family, I can't live with them and but I definitely can't live without them. They are there for me during tough times but also put me through some tough times. My family has been there since day one, literally. They have nurtured, protected and instilled within me tools that have helped me to navigate this cruel world. They helped mold me into the woman I AM today. They are my rock, my foundation, and my safety net. No matter what happens in life I know I will always have them to fall back on. I don't have to speak to them every day but they always seem to be there in the nick of time. Rather it is giving me a call, planning a gathering, or a kind gesture to make me feel loved, they always remind me that I AM never alone.

I AM LOVED!

Day 3

I AM Inspired!

Inspired = To be moved or guided by divine or supernatural influence

You are creative and can make things happen.

Today I read something from an entrepreneur that inspired me. She was a survivor of domestic violence and turned her pain into purpose by starting her own business helping other survivors. She reminded me that I AM more than a conqueror and I can achieve my goals if I go for it. I can't win if I don't show up for the battle. It was meant for me to come to it, so I could go through it, and help someone else live through it. Often I hear people say that I can't do this, I will never be that, I don't have the money for this, I don't know anything about that, what if it doesn't work, or I AM not ready for that. If you can think it, and you believe it, nothing can stop me from achieving it. I want to be an inspiration to someone. We overcome by hearing the testimony of others. Sometimes I AM embarrassed, ashamed, and think I AM the only one going through certain situations. However, when I speak out, I AM releasing the hold that situation had over me. When I AM walking in my purpose, I AM inspired! Just knowing that I have helped, touched, motivated, and encouraged one individual in my life inspires me.

I AM INSPIRED!

Day 4

I AM Beautiful!

*Beautiful = Possessing qualities that are pleasing;
delighting the senses or the mind*

*You are of a high and excellent standard of your own
kind.*

Today marks 6 months since I gave birth to me and my husband's first child. I have always been self-conscious about my appearance and weight. Once I became pregnant, I made sure that I did what I could to ensure that my body went through minimal changes in hopes of a quick recovery and bounce back. Thanks to my good genes and self-determination I was able to get back to my pre-pregnancy size clothing. Now that I was making public appearances, I went to an expo for Black Business owners and saw quite a few people that I had not seen in a while. Several people commented that I looked good and that it didn't look as if I even had a baby. After giving birth to a beautiful angel princess and being back to a new normal, hearing that comment felt good. It was a good feeling to be a mom, yet classy and sassy without showing any skin, without wearing tight clothes, or having unnatural amendments to my body. I had the glow even after giving birth, and my beauty exuded inside and out. Beauty is not just about what you wear, the style of your hair, or having big assets, but it radiates in your walk, your talk, your posture, and your personality.

I AM BEAUTIFUL!

Day 5

I AM Wiser!

Wiser = Marked by deep understanding, keen discernment, and a capacity for sound judgment

Everything that you have experienced has made you knowledgeable and given you information to make you an expert on the lessons you learned.

Today I was asked to do an interview to help someone collect data for a thesis paper. The interviewer asked me several questions pertaining to his research topic and I gave my raw and candid answers based on my knowledge and experiences. To conclude the interview, I was told that I AM very wise and that my answers provided a great deal of insight into the study. I have often been told that I AM wise beyond my years. I love being around the elderly, learning from their experiences, and listening to their stories. It is captivating to hear about others' successes as well as their mistakes. My motto is that a fool learns from his mistakes but a wise man learns from others so she doesn't have to make those mistakes. Everyone makes mistakes, but what separates the wise from the fools is choosing to take those lessons and make better choices in the future. I AM a big proponent of prevention and education. If I can save myself time, money, pain, and energy, and still get the same end results, I AM all for it. I like to think smart not hard. I strive to be wiser and better than yesterday, learning as I go so my tomorrow can be a better day.

I AM WISER!

Day 6

I AM Magnetic!

Magnetic = Having an unusual power or ability to attract

You have the power to attract the things that you want in life; good things will follow you and be drawn to you.

Today I attended a community event. While at the event supporting another organization, attendees approached me about my nonprofit organization, Cultivating Healthier Options In Communities Everywhere Int'l Inc. (C.H.O.I.C.E. Int'l Inc.), wanting to get more information about it. I met several people that had ventures, resources, or information that could serve as a collaboration or partner for my organization. All by being at the right place at the right time I connected with people and resources that I needed. It is something about having things come to you when you are not expecting it or looking for it. It is as if you are tapped into a force that pulls positive energy and resources to you attracted by your magnetic force. Some things and people will try to revolve around your magnetic field because they are attracted to what you are doing, your vision, and what you have to offer. However it does not mean that they are a good match resulting in repulsion. I AM a light that shines bright and bright lights often attract flies so I have to keep repellant, the Holy Ghost. When I am in tune with God I attract what He has in store for me.

I AM MAGNETIC!

Day 7

I AM Opportunistic!

Opportunistic = Taking advantage of expected and unexpected opportunities

You will have doors opens, paths cleared, and obstacles removed for opportunities that will benefit you, take advantage and seize the opportunity!

Today I could say I was proud to be a Mercer University Alumna. I must admit, that witnessing the Mercer Bears beat Duke University in what became the shock and underdog upset around the nation was pretty stellar. I wanted to be a part of the hype and wear my Mercer t-shirt pretending like I did not just jump on the band wagon. Then it dawned on me that I should host a watch party and have proceeds benefit my nonprofit. Talk about capitalizing on great opportunity. The drawback was I had one day to pull this off, market it, and get people to come. I started turning my wheels and things began to fall into place. The event was a success and what would have taken some people weeks or months to plan, took me a couple days to pull off. Opportunities are like revolving doors, they spin around and if I wait too long, I have missed that turn. Everyone gets a turn for the door to come around. The key is to jump in at the right time or get tripped up. Listening to Gods voice, following my instinct and developing my relationship with Him has helped me identify when opportunities are right for me and when it is my time to succeed.

I AM OPPORTUNISITC!

Day 8

I AM Admired!

Admired = To hold with high regard, esteem or to look up to someone

You are respected and held to a high reverence because you are a prize that has shown yourself approved by God.

Today I was hosting a watch party for the Mercer vs. Tennessee NCAA playoff game. I messaged a friend from college to invite her and her fiancé' over to cheer on the Bears and support of my organization. We engaged in conversation, catching up on lost time. Somewhere along the conversation we started talking about relationships and I advised her that in order to make a relationship work you can't rely on the partner to fulfill your every need. It's not their job to "complete" you. Seeking for someone else to make you whole will leave you feeling empty and lost if they leaver or don't live up to your expectations. They are placed in your life to be the physical impartation of God helping you in the mission for the kingdom. She said that she has always admired me for my faith. I felt admirable. We are called to be a living example set forth by Christ. If someone wants to see the living God, I want them to look at me and see Him, His example, and His model. To be admired for my faith means I AM honoring God by allowing Him to be edified and glorified. My admiration for God shines and I AM being the light He called me to be.

I AM ADMIRED!

Day 9
I AM Foreign!
Foreign = Of, in, or characteristic of something different than one's familiarities; strange

You are not of this world because you are a spiritual being with supernatural powers and extraterrestrial features.

Today I taught Zumba to a group of high school students. The youth gravitated towards me and were really excited about me coming to teach them Zumba. I quickly learned that young boys can be very mannish. As an adult female you have to watch them, yourself, your boundaries, and your demeanor. They have high levels of testosterone and hormones on 1,000. During one of our exercises, we were partnered up and there was an odd number of children. I partnered with the child that was left. While stretching, he asked where I was from and said that he could look at me and tell I AM not from the area. I inquired what he meant by that. He said I look foreign. What does that mean I asked? He pointed to the other girls and said they look like they are from here, they look ratchet. I was perplexed by the feelings they expressed towards their young black female peers. Was it because they are not looking for the common, around the way girl? I think it is very peculiar for girls to be seen and not heard. I AM in this world but not of this world.

I AM FOREIGN!

Day 10
I AM Winning!

Winning = To get a prize or reward by achieving victory in a fight, contest, or game

You may be in last place now but if you keep going and endure until the end you shall reap the reward.

Today I received a phone call from someone that wanted to compliment me on all my recent achievements. To have someone I respect as a mentor means that they see me coming up and I AM winning. Everyone wants to be noticed, to be recognized, and to be praised for their good deeds, works, and accomplishments. To be noticed means that you are doing something right.

Later that day, I received an email saying that I had won a family package to the Olympia Family Fun Center skating rink. I entered my name in the raffle at the Black Business Expo and I beat the odds. Winning this prize out of all the entries reminded me that I AM a winner in all aspects of life. It is so good to know that God chose me and I don't have to gamble, bet on anything, or risk anything to win his love, grace, and favor. He doesn't put our name in a bag, shake it up and use that to decide who is going to get blessings. With Him, no one loses. He has us all in His hand and we are all winners.

I AM WINNING!

Day 11
I AM Breathing!

Breathing = To inhale and exhale freely

May every breath you take in bring in renewed oxygen that flows through your lungs giving you the respiration needed to fully function. You will not hold on to bad oxygenated blood, exhale releasing the negativity that is built up and has circulated long enough through your body.

Today while driving, J Moss Psalms 150 came on the radio. With everything that I was going through I had come to a breaking point. I was tired of being strong, carrying the weight of the world on my shoulders, and bearing burdens on my own. I was overwhelmed and stressed. I was about to lose my mind pretending it was alright. While listening to the song, in the midst of my meltdown, I begin to praise God. I began to think about all that He has done for me. I began to reflect on all the good things, although it did not seem like there was much to be thankful for. I begin to smile. God saw fit for me to keep on so I must keep up the good fight. What didn't kill me, made me stronger. Weeping may endure for a night but joy comes in the morning. I began to have my own praise party down the highway. Despite everything that tried to make me give up and came to destroy me, I AM living. I AM surviving. I AM pressing through it. It didn't and will not defeat me. I AM making it and God is the reason for it. For that I can't help but praise Him. If He did nothing else, He allowed me to breath.

I AM BREATHING!

Day 12

I AM Complimented!

Complimented = To be presented with something as a mark of courtesy

You are good at what you do. You look dapper and have your own swag. You put the extra in extraordinary because you walk to the beat of your own drum and other people salute you. Even the haters are praising you and mad because you are just too good.

Today I dropped my daughter off at daycare. As I was leaving, one of the teachers was coming in. As she greeted me at the door she said, "Have a good day, I know you dressed your daughter up really pretty for pictures today. I can't wait to see her". As I walked out, it dawned on me that she likes the way I dress my daughter and more specifically is paying attention to the way I bring her to daycare. I took it as a compliment. As a mother, it is important that my child is decent and in order because she is a direct reflection of me. Babies are scrutinized at the expense of the parent. For example, someone may be smiling in your face, giving you a compliment saying your baby is so precious, but as soon as you leave they are saying 'did you see what she had that baby on'. As a mother it is important to take just as much pride in my child's appearance as I do my own. Raising a girl, I want to impart a sense of standards and daintiness within her so that she has a strong sense of self when she goes out in the world. When I carry myself with a certain poise and demeanor, people take notice. When I walk and dress with confidence, I AM silently speaking volumes.

I AM COMPLIMENTED!

Day 13
I AM Celebrated!

Celebrated = To observe a day or commemorate with a ceremony

You are greatly admired and people everywhere know of you because your birth, your life, was a day that changed the world and lives of many.

Today I realized that birthdays are a universal day for people to celebrate me. It's the one day that I feel like the most important person in the world. For my birthday, I was showered with gifts, cards, calls, and messages from many people. It is nice to be celebrated at least one day out of the year. It is good to know that you matter and people acknowledge the fact that your life has meaning to them. It made me really look at life from an external perspective. I began to ponder and compare the life I know I was given to live and the life that I have made for myself. I asked myself if they congruent. I questioned rather I AM where I should be at this point in life. I decided to not dwell on a fixated picture of what life should be like at this stage, but to celebrate everything up to that moment in life. I can celebrate or marinate in pity. The fact that I made it another year, the fact that I have life, is a testament that I AM accomplishing something. I may not be where I want to be, but at least I AM not where I used to be. I celebrate me, I celebrate life.

I AM CELEBRATED!

Day 14

I AM Committed!

Committed = Wholeheartedly dedicated, to pledge oneself to a job, activity, or cause

You are the person that everyone can depend on because you are loyal to family, friends, relationships, and positions.

Today I over committed myself to several engagements and meetings. After a long week, when Saturday came, I wanted to sleep in. I committed myself to getting up early and going to open a bank account for my nonprofit organization. As much as I wanted to stay in the bed for just thirty more minutes, I couldn't. I can't expect others to be committed to my organization or to me if I don't put forth the same effort and lead by example. Excellence and lazy don't mix. One delay would have thrown everything off. I had just enough time scheduled in between the many things I had to do today to drive from one place to next. By the time I got to the third meeting I was very tired. I really wanted to cancel. I pressed through and went on to meet my client. Honoring my commitments speaks volumes about my character and my passion. Plus, it keeps people committed to working with me knowing that I AM dependable and professional. Although tired, I learned that in order for me to be committed 100% to something, I can't over extend myself. I strive to give my all to everything I do and see it through. I know that my commitment will pay off.

I AM COMMITTED!

Day 15

I AM Caring!

Caring = Displaying kindness or concern for others
You look out for those that are not able to care for
themselves or in need. You show compassion for those
that need help and you often put the needs of others
before you own.

Today I met with one of my clients for a tutoring session. We were scheduled for a two hour session. Like clockwork, his mother drops him off right at the start time, and picks him up right at the end time. We finished all the projects and assignments on the syllabus for that day approximately 4 minutes ahead of schedule. Instead of leaving early or wasting time, I told the student that we were going to work the last four minutes because his mother pays for him to learn. The student's reply was, "finally a tutor who cares". Children can tell when someone truly cares and genuinely believes in them. I think that many of the behaviors that children exhibit in the classroom come from their lack of validation from a significant adult that pushes them to achieve and do better. Children need guidance. Every child deserves a quality education. Some children don't put forth the effort to learn because no one has pushed them or reinforced their ability to succeed if they try. An investment in our youth is an investment in our future. We can't afford not to make a deposit. Every child needs someone that truly cares for them and someone to hold them accountable.

I AM CARING!

Day 16

I AM Fit!

Fit = Of suitable quality, standard, or type to meet the required purpose

You are physically in good shape and as a result you will have emotional and mental benefits from taking care of your temple.

Today I was really feeling myself. Have you ever just looked in the mirror and said 'dang, if I wasn't me I would want to be me! Or I AM so fine and sexy!' I know everyone has done that twirl with a spin, then striking a pose and dancing in the mirror with your best outfit on. Today I was loving me some me. Especially since after having my daughter, I lost all the baby weight and then some, I was in my zone. I AM below my pre pregnancy weight and the weight that I did gain made everything thick and curvy in the right places. As a mom, it definitely was a boost to feel good again, and feel like I didn't lose my body after having a child. It does take work though. Breast feeding helped me to lose a lot of the post weight. Not to mention, lifting and carrying a car seat everywhere got my biceps pumped. Eventually I was able to establish a routine where I could work out for 20 to 30 minutes. Sometimes it included the baby, walking her in the stroller around the neighborhood, or doing a quick television routine while she slept. It certainly helped give me energy which I could never find enough of with a new baby. Exercise does a body good.

I AM FIT!

Day 17

I AM Respectful!

Respectful = To show consideration or regard for someone or something

You give respect to others and respect is given unto you. You were raised with good manners, morals, and standards.

Today I was getting out of my car in the parking lot at the grocery store and I heard a big boom boom thump thump rattling sound as a vehicle was pulling up. The music was playing so loudly the whole county could have heard it. In light of the Jordan Davis situation that resulted in the young man losing his life reportedly because the music was too loud, I felt it was my civil duty to talk to these young men about respect. I asked the guys why the music was so loud. One guy said, as he pointed to the elaborately decorated vehicle, that it was promotion for him. I said oh ok and went on. I understand we have liberty to play what we want, but there is a level of respect for others that should accompany that freedom. I will admit when I was a teenager that I was privileged to have my first car equipped with great speakers. I would bump my music loud when I was passing by others to draw attention to myself and my flashy accessories. As I became older I became aware that being respectful is not just saying yes ma'am and no sir. It involves being considerate of others, their feelings, their rights, and their thoughts.

I AM RESPECTFUL!

Day 18

I AM Giving!

Giving = The transfer of something without expecting anything in return

You are generous and have an abundance of blessings that you share with those that are less fortunate than you. You are always receiving because your hands are open and not closed.

Today a coworker came by my desk and asked for some cash to buy lunch. She had locked her purse in her drawer and security was not able to find the master key for her cabinet. I willingly told her I would give her what cash I had, as I typically don't carry cash. As I went to my car to get the money I was thinking to myself, this is the same person that would otherwise walk by my desk and not speak to me. However I AM giving and I don't want to treat her like she treats me. I give out of the kindness of my heart. I give because I AM blessed to be a blessing. I haven't done anything so great to deserve everything that has been given to me. Fortunately, God sees fit to keep blessing me. It is easy to give when I AM not in need or when I expect to get paid back. The challenge comes when you don't have it to spare or when that person hasn't treated you fair. I have learned that ultimately God will supply my needs and thus I allow Him to use me to supply the needs of others. I always give with a cheerful heart, and with a heart of thankfulness. I know that is why I AM never the beggar and continuously able to give and have enough to live.

I AM GIVING!

Day 19
I AM Intellectual!

Intellectual = One who engages in critical study, thought and reflection about the reality of society, proposes solutions for the normative problems of society, and by such discourse , gains authority by public opinion
You have very bright ideas that are so enormous that they are on a global scale. You are an expert in your field and others look to you because you are knowledgeable and credible in your information.

Today I had an enlightening conversation with someone. Eleanor Roosevelt once said, "Great minds talk about ideas, average minds talk about events, and small minds talk about people." Generally when speaking to people, I cater my conversation to defray from gossip and spreading business that is not my own. If the conversation does not serve the purpose of me learning something, me teaching someone, or anything helpful, I tend to cut it short. I AM careful in discussing my ideas with certain people because sometimes they are too big for certain people to understand. Some people I avoid talking to altogether because I know what comes out of their mouth is going to be stupidity and of no real value to me. If the conversation doesn't elevate me, invoke me to think, or question my present status, then I am usually quiet. I don't dabble much in small talk. If you are not trying to educate yourself, read a book, learn something, think outside the box, and broaden your horizons, I have to set sail and leave your shore because the waters are too shallow and I AM a deep thinker. I AM on a quest to learn. Knowledge is power.

I AM INTELLECTUAL!

Day 20
I AM Covered!

Covered = To place something upon or over so as to protect or conceal

You are shielded from danger and guarded from any weapon that tries to form against you.

Today I headed out of the country to Jamaica to celebrate my birthday. I had been fore warned not to bring or charge credit cards because it will cost you more money internationally. I didn't have to budget a lot of money for expenses since my food, beverages, activities, lodging, transportation from the resort to tourist spots, and air fare were all included in the package. All I had to do was check in and start the fantastic voyage. Nothing could ruin my fun. Well almost nothing, except the long line at the security check point. I missed my flight. I thought that my trip was ruined. I prayed that I could still make it. Well not only did I get on the next flight, which arrived in Montego Bay earlier than my original flight was planned for, I also got to sit in first class. The person that sat next to me on the plane happened to be a native of Jamaica and gave me some Jamaican money after I told her I was going to celebrate my birthday. She said whatever you need, I got you covered. She gave me her number and tips on what to do while in Jamaica. It is so nice to know that wherever I go, God has angels covering me. All things work together for my good and my protection.

I AM COVERED!!

Day 21

I AM Brave!

Brave = Ready to endure of face danger or pain; showing courage

You are not afraid to go after what you want. Nothing can stop you or hold you back from leaping into the unknown and conquering your deepest fears but you. You will get out of your own way.

Today I lived my life like it was golden. I couldn't possibly be in Jamaica and not get in the beautiful see through, aquamarine water. So, I went snorkeling. The daring part was that I couldn't swim. The old me would have never been in the ocean snorkeling, swimming, or trying to find Nemo. As I took the first step to get off the boat I was cool. As I took the second step, I started breathing a little faster. By the time I took the third step I was calling for my mama. When I put my foot in the water, I immediately hopped back onto the boat. The captain of the boat said in his Jamaican accent, "Princess, are you ok?" Shaking my head no, I asked him if he could escort me. He jumped in the water, attempting to escort me but I was so panicked that I was making it difficult for him to hold me and keep himself composed. I managed to stick my head under the water. I was able to see a school of fish and beautiful, colorful coral reef. It was the coolest and prettiest thing I had ever seen. The water was so clear but very salty. All things considered, I think I did a good job of facing my fears.

I AM BRAVE!

Day 22

I AM Calm

Calm = Not showing or feeling nervousness, anger, or other emotions

You are in pleasant state free from turmoil and storms. You have an inner peace that allows you to have quietness in the thunder and keep dry in the rain.

Today I sat on the beautiful beach of Jamaica and basked in the ambiance of the ocean. I sat just listening to the waves as they played patty cake with the soft sands on the shore. It was such a soothing and therapeutic sound that I felt my melatonin levels rising and I fell asleep on the beach. I was in a state of calmness and relaxation. With each wave that came in I released a problem or concern and let it wash away as the wave carried my cares into the endless ocean. When the waves came back in I released another issue and this continued until I was content and care free. I was at peace. I released my stress. Ironically I coach people on how to manage stress yet I was at a high stress level prior to this trip. I finally put into play some of the tips I give my clients. Stress can be managed by stimulating the senses. The ocean stimulates the sense of sound. Getting to a place of calmness so that I can think straight and clearly is good for distressing. Finding a sense of peace, something that centers me and takes me away from everything is one way I connect with the spirit of serenity. Once I AM there I release and let go of everything. When I do this I find myself calm and relaxed.

I AM CALM!

Day 23

I AM Thrifty

*Thrifty = Using money and other resources carefully and
not wastefully*

*You are able to do a lot with a little. You never lack
anything because you make the most out of everything
you are given and are resourceful.*

Today I went to the post office to send off a package. The representative asked me if she could help and I told her that I was trying to mail something small. She suggested that I get a box which was twice as much as the envelope. I declined her suggestion and said that I would get the envelope if it will do the same job for half the price. She then called me cheap because I opted not to get the box and said that I should not send a package in an envelope. I said that you call it cheap, I call it frugal. I took the envelope, paid for the package to be shipped and left. I think that sometimes it does not require paying extra money when the same objective can be achieved and I can still have coins in my pocket to do a little something extra. Who doesn't like to save money? Or better yet, who likes to give money away? If you raised your hand on that last question please mail a check my way. Thanks! People who have lots of money spend it as if they were poor and people with no money spend it as if they were rich. This is how many millionaires become rich, and many poor people stay in poverty. I like to cut out unnecessary expenses even if I have money to spare.

I AM THRIFTY!

Day 24

I AM Still

Still = In deep silence; not moving or making a sound
You are in a place where God wants to speak to you and
tell you everything He has in store for you, everything He
has planned for you, and show you the vision plainly and
clearly. The only way you can hear it is to be still and let
Him move and work.

Today I realized that sometimes I need to slow down and be still. I AM a very busy person and often I get lost in thinking that being busy is equivalent to being accomplished and effective. Sometimes I have to sit down and really get clarity on what it is that I need to be doing and devoting my time and energy towards. It is better to do one thing great than to have ten things going on and all of them only get 10% of my best. Although I can do several things at once because I AM that gifted, I AM learning to operate in excellence in all that I do which requires me to have a plan, prepare, and be intentional with every move.

When I AM still I can hear the voice of God plainly without distractions or temptation and I know exactly when and how to move next. When I AM still, I have time to collect myself, embrace the moment, assess the situation, look at the big picture, and fine tune small details. I don't want to make mistakes and I don't like wasting time, energy, money, or efforts. The best way to reduce error is to be still and let God be my compass.

I AM STILL!

Day 25

I AM Connected

Connected = Bring together or in contact so that a real or notional link is established

You are the direct heir of royalty and as a result you are connected to everyone and everything you need to achieve your purpose and to sustain.

Today I connected the dots. We are all one spirit. To truly tap into the oneness and connectedness brings unlimited power, abundance, and overflow of endless possibilities at my fingertips. Together we can all achieve more. God perfectly orchestrated for someone to have a piece of what I need to complete the puzzle of His perfect will for my life. When I connect myself with others I AM empowered, inspired, and enabled to accomplish my purpose. Sometimes this connection is for a moment, a season, or a lifetime, but it is a necessary link to help me along the journey and circle of life that continues long after I AM gone. I AM just connecting the dots and doing my part. Connections aren't broken, you just move further along in the chain. It is one source from which all energy flows that connects us and it can't be created nor destroyed. Never break ties with people that you may need in the future because life usually comes full circle and you see those links again. Sometimes connections that were made at one point in life may not have meaning or make sense until later in life. It is important to foster connections because we all need somebody.

I AM CONNECTED!

Day 26

I AM Boosterish

Boosterish = Supporting or promoting something enthusiastically and often uncritically
You do not stand in the way of others because you are so confident in your own lane that you can support others and not hate on them. You are happy where you are and happy for them where they are going.

Today I gave my support to a worthy cause. I enjoy giving back and helping others achieve their dreams. I don't mind teaching and lending my expertise to others that want to follow in my footsteps or create a path of their own. I don't get jealous, envious, or mad when I see others doing well. In fact, I support them with all that I have. One day they may be in a position to help me get to a higher level. One of my protégés is in the process of applying to college. He asked me to write him a letter of recommendation since he often volunteers with my nonprofit organization. I humbly agreed to the honor to be a part of his future and preparation for success. He said that he has plans to make his family proud and buy his grandmother a house. He added that he was going to give back to C.H.O.I.C.E. Int'l Inc. and donate funds when he gets rich. It is a great feeling to be able to genuinely support others helping them achieve their optimal potential. As I go higher on my ladder to success, my passion is to lift up others and take others with me on this journey. There is room for everyone to be great and get a piece of the pie.

I AM BOOSTERISH!

Day 27

I AM Prayerful!

Prayerful = A person giving devout solemn request of a hope or wish

Your cries and praises are heard on high. All of your worries, burdens, and requests shall be added and given unto you if you ask the Lord's help and take it to Him in prayer.

Today I was having one of those days. All I could do was pray. I literally could not move. The only thing I could do was to call on the name of Jesus. I began to seek Him. I much as I tried to cast my cares part of me was still holding on. It had paralyzed me and all I could do was lay and weep at his feet. I needed Him. At first I was praying all the time and as I went along and as things were seemingly looking up, I stopped praying as much as I did when I was in the thick of the fire. I was quickly reminded that prayer should not be just when I AM in trouble. Prayer is necessary for a healthy and vital relationship with God. I need to talk to Him every day. I must let Him know when I AM thinking of Him, that I love Him, and that He's everything to me. Praying does not accomplish its goal if I AM still holding on to the very thing that I went to pray about. I have to let it go and leave it in the prayer closet, close the door, and lock it. When I pray something has to happen. Things are bound in the earthly realm, things are loosed in the spiritual realm, and a shaking starts to occur. It may not unfold right then but its working, the answer may not be clear but it's working.

I AM PRAYERFUL!

Day 28

I AM Closer

Closer = In a position so as to be very near to someone or something

You are almost at the finish line and your season is here. You are closer to discovering your purpose. You are closer to manifesting your destiny. All you have to do is make it over and it is yours.

Today I received a word that was right on time. The moment that things are going well for me, the enemy intentionally plants people and things to set me up in attempt to deter me from my destiny. There are very few things that can knock me off my course and distract me from my mission. I try to stay focused and generally I don't let things rock my boat. However, this season the weeds, vultures, rats, deer, and everything that loves fresh harvested produce was lurking in my garden. Right before I could reap what I had sown, the critters got to it. Literally everyday was sunny, the temperature was perfect, the grass was green, and the crops were promising. One thing I do know is that if I did not have a crop that was going to reap everything God promised me, the enemy would have never tried to attack it. I know I AM closer and for that I AM going to keep praising through this storm even if it wipes out all my crops. I AM going to plant some more. I AM going to keep watering and staying hopeful because the enemy will get tired before I do. I will reap my harvest in due season.

I AM CLOSER!

Day 29

I AM Backed

Backed = To support or confirm; reinforce

You have the hand of God on your back and no matter which way you lean, sway, or trip, you will not fall, hit the bottom or stumble because He has your back, your front, and your side.

Today at work a colleague and I were conversing about how some people on the job are cut throat. My colleague gave me an encouraging word. She told me, " you don't need these people to have your back, God has your back and that is all you need to succeed." This was a message in more ways than one. To know that God has my back and that no matter whom or what tries to push me down, tear me apart or destroy me, they can't get to me without going through Him first. The wind may blow but I will stand firm like a tree planted by the rivers of water, I shall not be moved. Every promotion, every raise, every assignment, and every project is backed by God. Therefore, everything I put my name on shall prosper. Every effort shall be successful. Even when others try to get credit for work I did, without the seal of approval from God, no CEO, president, or supervisor can get what belongs to me. It is an amazing feeling to know that with every move God is my co-signer. His credit history is clean. Everything I apply for is already mine because God has my back.

I AM BACKED!

Day 30

I AM Stronger

Stronger = Able to withstand great force or pressure; having the power or ability to move heavy weights or perform other physical demanding tasks

You are a survivor and everything that you have beat and defeated has made you more resilient and able to withstand the next thing that comes your way!

Today I AM feeling stronger. I know that Jesus is strengthening me as I continue on my journey. When a person lifts weights, especially something challenging and out of their comfort zone, typically they have a spotter to assist them just in case the weights get to be too much to handle alone. Having a spotter is not a sign of weakness; in fact it is smart to have a spotter to ensure you don't hurt yourself. As the person gets stronger and adds more weight, the muscles have to get accustomed to the new strain. As the person stretches, the muscles may give out, may spasm, or may pull in awkward directions. My muscles were definitely stretched these past 30 days but I AM stronger. I AM getting in shape for the fight of my life. It is comforting to know that God is my spotter. I AM never alone. It is through Christ that strengthens me that I can withstand anything. Even in my weakest times, God is always with me to show me that His strength can endure anything. At times when I thought I would fall, break, crumble, and stumble, God reached down and held me up. There are days when I AM weak, weary, and want to give up but God strengthens me and I carry on.

I AM STRONGER!

THE END

You know my story; you see my glory; now take the challenge for yourself! I look forward to hearing your story and seeing your glory as well.

www.ingramcontent.com/pod-product-compliance
Lightning Source LLC
LaVergne TN
LVHW011338080426
835513LV00006B/420